Weight Watchers Freestyle Cookbook 2019

Start Healing Your Body With Healthy & Delicious WW Smart Points Recipes

By
Desmond Silas

TABLE OF CONTENTS

CAJUN CAT FISH RECIPE

OVEN FRIED FISH WEIGHT WATCHERS

BLACKENED ZUCCHINI WRAPPED FISH

FISH AND SHRIMP STEW

PARCHMENT BAKED FISH

SLIMMING GINGER STEAMED FISH

ONE PAN BAKED TERIYAKI SALMON

SHRIMP SCAMPI

BLACKENED FISH TACOS WITH CABBAGE MANGO SLAW

DIJON FISH FILLETS

FISH TACO RICE BOWLS

COCONUT FRIED FISH

BRAZILIAN FISH STEW

BLACKENED CATFISH OVER CAJUN RICE RECIPE

SPINACH AND FETA STUFFED TILAPIA

PARMESAN CRUSTED TILAPIA

PAN-SEARED TILAPIA IN TOMATO BASIL SAUCE

FISH PIE WITH CHEESY MASH

MOROCCAN FISH TAGINE WITH GINGER & SAFFRON

FRIED WHOLE FISH WITH TOMATILLO SAUCE

CHUNKY FISH AND SWEET POTATO CURRY

MEXICAN BAKED FISH

STEAMED FISH WITH LIME AND GARLIC RECIPE

SAUTÉED FLOUNDER WITH MINT AND TOMATOES

BROILED TILAPIA

GRILLED MISO-GLAZED COD

BAKED SALMON PUTTANESCA

GRILLED TUNA PROVENCAL

LEMON-HERB ROASTED SALMON

NUT-CRUSTED MAHI-MAHI

Introduction

The Weight Watchers plan is based upon the idea that dieting is only one part of a healthy lifestyle. The program stresses the importance of overall mental and physical health and well-being.

The Weight Watchers system works on a "points" basis. Points are based on the calories in a product making the plan seem more exotic. While it's a relatively simple concept, reducing calories is a key ingredient in dropping pounds.

Weight Watchers adjusts with famous trackers. On the off chance that you claim a Fit bit for weight reduction or utilize another gadget or weight reduction application like Jawbone, Within, Misfit, Garmin Vivo fit, Apple Health, or Map-My-Run, you can match up your information to Weight Watchers so the majority of your weight reduction information is kept up and can be overseen in one place.

This **weight watchers freestyle cookbook 2019 will deliver** top easy & delicious smart points recipes for your free lifestyle. The recipes are easy to follow and can be used by anyone regardless of their background.

RECIPE :- COCONUT CHICKEN WITH PINA COLADA DIP

Servings: 4

Total Time: 35mins, Prep Time: 5mins, Cook Time: 30mins

Ingredients:

- ❖ 1 - tbsp fresh lime juice
- ❖ 1 - tbsp hot pepper sauce
- ❖ 14 - oz can light coconut milk
- ❖ 1 - lb boneless skinless boneless
- ❖ ¾ - cup bread crumbs
- ❖ ½ - cup sweetened flaked coconut
- ❖ ½ - tsp salt
- ❖ ¼ - tsp black pepper
- ❖ 3 - oz crushed canned pineapple
- ❖ 3 - oz fat-free sour cream
- ❖ 4 - oz pina colada nonalcoholic drink mixer

Instructions:

- ✓ Preheat broiler to 400 tiers F (205 levels C).
- ✓ For the coconut fowl: Mix lime juice, warm pepper sauce, and light coconut drain collectively in a huge resalable plastic percent.
- ✓ Include bird and seal. Marinate inside the icebox for half hours, turning the percent every so often.

- ✓ Join bread scraps, chipped coconut, salt, and dark pepper in a shallow bowl. Expel fowl from the marinade and put off the overabundance. Coat fowl one piece at once within the breadcrumb blend, at that factor placed on a preparing sheet showered with cooking splash.
- ✓ Coat the highest factor of the chook with a cooling splash.
- ✓ Warmth for 30 minutes or until the factor that the hen is in no way, shape or form again blood red in the center and the juices run clean.
- ✓ Warmth for 30 minutes or until the factor that the hen is in no way, shape or form again red in the center and the juices run clean.
- ✓ For the pina colada dive: In a little bowl, by and large all in all combo pineapple, sharp cream, and pina colada nonalcoholic drink blender.
- ✓ Present with the flying creature.

Nutritional Information per Serving

Calories: 301g, Fat 8g, Carbs 27g, Sugars 11g, Protein 28g

Points Values: 11

Servings: 8

Total Time: 8hrs 10mins, Prep Time: 10mins, Cook Time: 8hrs

Ingredients:

- ❖ 12 - oz boneless, skinless chicken breast
- ❖ 1 3/8 - oz chili seasoning mix
- ❖ 1 - qt canned tomatoes
- ❖ 15 - oz corn
- ❖ 15 - oz kidney beans
- ❖ 1 - green bell pepper
- ❖ 1 - onion
- ❖ ½ - cup salsa

Instructions:

- ✓ Splash a nonstick skillet with cooking shower and burn the fowl.
- ✓ Include chicken, stew flavoring mixture, tomatoes, corn, kidney beans, green Chile pepper, onion, and salsa to a simmering pot.
- ✓ Cover and prepare dinner on Low for 6 to 8 hours.

Nutritional Information per Serving:

Calories: 160g, Fat 2g, Carbs 24g, Sugars 7g, Protein 14g

Points Values: 4

RECIPE :- CHICKEN AND CHEESE CASSEROLE

Servings: 8

Total Time: 55mins, Prep Time: 10mins, Cook Time: 45mins

Ingredients:

- ❖ 2 - cup macaroni
- ❖ 2 - cup boneless, skinless chicken breast
- ❖ 2 - cup cream of mushroom soup
- ❖ 2 - cup skim milk
- ❖ 8 - oz low-fat cheddar cheese

Instructions:

- ✓ Preheat broiler to 350 degrees F (175 tiers C).
- ✓ In an expansive goulash dish, join macaroni, chook bosom, and cream of mushroom soup, skim drain, and cheddar, mixing admirably.
- ✓ Cover and warmth for 35 - 45 minutes.
- ✓ Expel cover and prepare for 10-15mins longer.

Nutritional Information per Serving
Calories: 153g, Fat 4g, Carbs 16g, Sugars 1g, Protein 12g
Points Values: 5

Servings: 16

Total Time: 50mins, Prep Time: 30mins, Cook Time: 20mins

Ingredients:

Lightened Up Alfredo Sauce:

- ❖ 1 - tablespoon unsalted butter
- ❖ 1 - tablespoon finely minced shallots
- ❖ 2 - teaspoons minced garlic
- ❖ 1 - tablespoon white whole wheat flour
- ❖ 1 - cup skim milk
- ❖ 2 - ounces ⅓ less fat cream cheese
- ❖ ¾ - cup shredded Parmesan cheese
- ❖ ½ - teaspoon salt

Chicken Alfredo Pizza:

- ❖ 3 - cups low-sodium chicken broth
- ❖ 1 - pound boneless
- ❖ 3 - slices baked center cut bacon
- ❖ 1 ½ - cups Lightened Up Alfredo
- ❖ 2 - cups baby spinach
- ❖ ¼ - cup shredded reduced-fat mozzarella cheese
- ❖ ¼ - teaspoon red pepper flakes

Instructions:

Alfredo sauce:

- ✓ In a bit pan over medium warmth, dissolve the margarine and cook dinner the shallots and garlic till the point that the shallots are sensitive and the garlic is fragrant, about 2mins.
- ✓ Mix in the flour and cook dinner for is 30 seconds until the spread, shallots, and garlic turn into a thick glue. Race in the drain and keep dashing for round 2mins, till the factor that the drain starts off-evolved to thicken. Mix in the cream cheddar, Parmesan cheddar, and salt and blend until the point that the cheeses dissolve, for round 2 minutes.

To make the pizza:
- ✓ In a stockpot over high warmth, heat 3 measures of the bird juices to the factor of boiling.
- ✓ Add the hen bosoms to the bubbling water and prepare dinner for 20-25 minutes or till the point that the fowl are never again red within the middle.
- ✓ Expel the bosoms from the water and set on a plate to chill. At the point whilst cool enough to contact, shred the chook bosoms with a fork.
- ✓ Preheat the broiler to 400°F. Line a rimmed heating sheet with thwart, and vicinity a cooling rack over the thwart.
- ✓ Lay the bacon strips at the rack, and put together for 10-15 minutes, until wanted freshness.
- ✓ In the period in-between, deliver down the broiler temperature to 350° F. Shower a getting ready sheet with nonstick cooking splashes and famous the batter to about a 10x14-inch rectangular form. Pre-heat the pizza aggregate hull for 6mins.
- ✓ Uniformly spread 1½ measures of the readied Alfredo sauce at the pre-heated hull, leaving round 1 inch of the outside layer edges without sauce.
- ✓ Layer the spinach, bird, bacon, cheddar and purple pepper drops over the sauce.
- ✓ Heat the pizza once more to dissolve the cheddar, around four minutes.

Nutritional Information per Serving
Calories: 400g, Fat 18g, Carbs 34g, Sugar 5g, Protein 27g
Points Values: 12

Servings: 5
Total Time: 25mins, Prep time: 10mins, Cook time: 15mins

Ingredients:

- ❖ 3 - cups low-sodium chicken broth
- ❖ 2 - dried bay leaves
- ❖ 1 - pound boneless, skinless chicken breasts
- ❖ 8 -ounce crushed pineapple
- ❖ 10.5 -ounce no-sugar-added mandarin oranges
- ❖ 2 - stalks celery
- ❖ ½ - cut shredded carrots
- ❖ ¼ - cup sliced almonds
- ❖ 2 - green onions
- ❖ ½ - teaspoon salt
- ❖ ¼ - teaspoon black pepper
- ❖ 10 - Boston Bib lettuce leaves
- ❖ ¼ - cup plain, nonfat Greek yogurt
- ❖ ¼ - cup light mayonnaise
- ❖ 1 - tablespoon brown sugar
- ❖ 1 - teaspoon sesame seeds
- ❖ 1 - teaspoon garlic powder
- ❖ 1 - teaspoon ground ginger

Instructions:

- ✓ In a medium stock pot, convey the chicken juices to a stew. Include the inlet leaves and chicken and stew secured for 15 minutes, flipping over at the midway stamp. The inside temperature should peruse 165°F.
- ✓ Dispose of the cove leaves and save the chicken on a plate until cool enough to contact, at that point shred and put aside.
- ✓ In a little bowl, whisk together the dressing fixings; put aside.
- ✓ In a huge bowl, consolidate the destroyed chicken, pineapple, mandarin oranges, celery, carrots, almonds, green onions, salt, and pepper. Include the put aside dressing, and hurl with tongs to equally consolidate.
- ✓ To serve, put ½ glass chicken plate of mixed greens in every lettuce leaf.

Nutritional Information per Serving

Calories: 245g, Fat 8g, Carbs 21g, Sugar 12g, Protein 23g

Points Values: 7

RECIPE :- SKINNY HAWAIIAN BBQ CHICKEN CUPS

Servings 12

Total Time: 35mins, Prep time: 5mins, Cook time: 30mins

Ingredients:

- ❖ 1 - pound boneless, skinless chicken breasts
- ❖ 8 -ounce crushed pineapple
- ❖ ½ - cup low-sugar BBQ sauce
- ❖ ½ - teaspoon dry ginger
- ❖ ½ - teaspoon salt
- ❖ 1 - cup reduced-fat mild shredded cheddar cheese
- ❖ 3.5 -inch wonton wrappers
- ❖ 2 - green onions

Instructions:

- ✓ Preheat the stove to 350°F and bathe a bit biscuit tin with a nonstick cooking splash, put aside.
- ✓ Place the hen bosoms in a pot sufficiently vast to preserve them all, and fill the pot with enough water to cowl the bird by round 1-2 inches. Add 2 dried sound leaves to the water and heat to the point of boiling over high warmth.

- ✓ Cover the pot and lessen the warmth to low. Stew the chicken for 15 minutes, or till the factor when the inward temperature of the thickest piece of the bosom peruses 165° F.
- ✓ Utilizing tongs, keep the chicken on a plate. When its miles cool sufficient to touch, shred it.
- ✓ In a medium blending dish with tongs, hurl together the destroyed bird, pineapple, BBQ sauce, ginger, salt, and ½ measure of the cheddar.
- ✓ To installation the wonton glasses, placed them within the readied biscuit tin, with the corners marginally overhanging.
- ✓ Spoon a loading tablespoon of the chook combination into every wonton glass, and uniformly top all of them with the rest of the ½ degree of cheddar.
- ✓ Prepare until the point while the cheddar is softened and the rims of the wonton wrappers are amazing, 10-12mins.
- ✓ Topping the highest factor of the glasses with the cut inexperienced onions and serve warm.

Nutritional Information per Serving

Calories: 133g, Fat 3g, Carbs 14g, Sugar 4g, Protein 12g

Points Values: 3

Servings: 4

Total Time: 60mins, Prep time: 10mins, Cook Time: 50mins

Ingredients:

- ❖ 1 - pound boneless, skinless chicken breasts
- ❖ ⅓ - cup plus 2 teaspoons cornstarch
- ❖ 2 - tablespoon extra virgin olive oil
- ❖ 8 -ounce juice-packed pineapple chunks
- ❖ ¼ - cup reduced-sugar ketchup
- ❖ 2 - tablespoons rice vinegar
- ❖ 1 - tablespoon less-sodium soy sauce
- ❖ 1 - teaspoon minced garlic
- ❖ 1 - teaspoon stevia
- ❖ ⅛ - teaspoon red pepper flakes
- ❖ 1 - small onion
- ❖ 1 - red bell pepper
- ❖ 1 - yellow bell pepper
- ❖ 3 - green onions

Instructions:

- ✓ Preheat the stove to 350°F. Coat an 11x7-inch heating dish with a cooking splash.
- ✓ Place the bird and ⅓ degree of the cornstarch in a big resalable percent. Seal and shake the sack multiple instances to uniformly coat the hen.
- ✓ In a wok or substantial skillet, warm the olive oil over medium-high warm temperature. Include the fowl in a solitary layer and cook dinner the chicken until seared all

completed but not cooked thru, 1 to 2mins, turning the fowl every now and then. Expel from the warm temperature.

✓ Deplete the pineapple and save the juice for the sauce.
✓ In a little bowl, whisk together the held pineapple juice, ketchup, rice vinegar, soy sauce, garlic, Stevie, pink pepper portions, and last 2 teaspoons of the cornstarch.
✓ Place the caramelized chicken pieces within the base of the readied heating dish. Include the pineapple lumps, onion, and crimson and yellow Chile peppers. Pour the sauce similarly over the chicken and greens.
✓ Cover the preparing dish freely with thwart and warmth till the factor when the sauce is foaming and the chook is cooked via round 45 minutes. Blend the chook blend and pivot the dish the front to return a part of the manner via the heating time to assure that it chefs equitably.
✓ Serve decorated with the inexperienced onions.

Nutritional Information per Serving

Calories: 294g, Fat 10g, Carbs 29g, Sugar 13g, Protein 24g

Points Values: 8

Servings: 12

Total Time: 30mins, Prep Time: 10mins, Cook Time: 20mins

Ingredients:

- ❖ 8 - oz low fat cream cheese
- ❖ ⅛ - cup buffalo sauce
- ❖ 2 - cups cooked and shredded chicken
- ❖ 12 - small flour tortillas

Sauce:

- ❖ Fat free Ranch Dressing

Instructions:

- ✓ Preheat stove to 425 degrees F.
- ✓ Blend cream cheddar and wild ox sauce until the point that very much joined.
- ✓ Mix in chicken until the point when very much consolidated.
- ✓ Place 2-3 Tablespoons of blend spread into a thin line onto focal point of a flour tortilla.
- ✓ Place on daintily lubed treat sheet and rehash for outstanding taquitos.
- ✓ When taquitos are masterminded on treat sheet, softly shower the finish with a cooking splash.
- ✓ Prepare at 425 degrees F for 15-20 minutes or until the point when taquitos are brilliant darker.

Calories: 148g, Fat 8.06g. Carbs 8.32g, Sugar 0.04g, Protein 13.65g

Points Values: 4

RECIPE :- BUFFALO CHICKEN LASAGNA

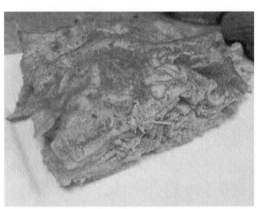

Servings: 8

Total Time: 1hr 40mins, Prep Time: 25mins, Cook Time: 1hr 15mins

Ingredients:

- ❖ 8 - Whole Wheat Lasagna Noodles
- ❖ 1 - lb. skinless chicken breast
- ❖ 3 - cups crushed tomatoes
- ❖ 1 - cup Franks Buffalo Wing Sauce
- ❖ 1 - ½ - cups water
- ❖ 15 - oz low fat ricotta cheese
- ❖ ½ - cup egg substitutes
- ❖ 8 - oz of pepper jack

Instructions:

1. Preheat stove to 350 degrees and daintily splash a 9×13 heating dish with nonstick cooking shower. In a little blending dish, join ricotta cheddar and egg substitute and put aside.
2. In an alternate blending dish, consolidate water, pulverized tomatoes, wing sauce, and chicken.

3. Spread roughly one measure of the sauce and chicken blend over the base of the skillet, and organize four of the noodle over the sauce.
4. Spread a layer of sauce over the noodles and after that spread a layer of the ricotta blend over the sauce.
5. Include another layer of noodles and rehash the procedure until the point that you end with a layer of simply the sauce and chicken blend. Cover with aluminum thwart and heat for an hour.
6. Expel dish from the stove, sprinkle blue cheddar disintegrates or pepper jack cheddar equitably preposterous.
7. Place back in the broiler revealed and heat for an extra 15 minutes.

Nutritional Information per Serving

Calories: 240g, Fat 10g, Carbs 15g, Sugars 8g, Protein 21g

Points Values: 6

RECIPE :- ONE- POT CHEESY CHICKEN RICE

Servings: 8

Total Time: 40mins, Prep Time: 15mins, Cook Time: 25mins

Ingredients:

- ❖ 1 – 1.5 - lbs lean ground chicken
- ❖ ½ - yellow onion
- ❖ 1 - tablespoon canola oil
- ❖ 1½ - cups uncooked instant brown rice
- ❖ 1 - teaspoon cumin
- ❖ ½ - teaspoon salt
- ❖ ½ - teaspoon garlic powder
- ❖ ½ - teaspoon chili powder
- ❖ 2 - cups low sodium chicken broth
- ❖ 14.5 - oz jar salsa
- ❖ 1 - cup corn kernels

- ❖ 1 - cup canned black beans
- ❖ 1 - Roma tomato
- ❖ ¾ - cup shredded cheddar cheese
- ❖ 1 - avocado
- ❖ 1 - green onion
- ❖ Fresh cilantro

Instructions:

- ✓ Add oil to an extensive skillet over medium-high warmth. Include the floor hen and split it up a bit with a wood spoon. Include the diced onion and prepare dinner until the factor that the chook has sautéed and the onion is translucent.
- ✓ Move the bird and onion over to the other facet of the skillet and shower barely more oil at the vacant facet. Include the uncooked rice and hurl it round fast to toast it.
- ✓ Blend inside the flavors, chook stock, salsa, corn, and dark beans. Convey the fluids to a stew and after that decrease the warm temperature to low. Cover and prepare dinner for 18mins or till the point when rice is sensitive and fluid has retained.
- ✓ Taste the rice and adjust flavoring for your taking part in. Sprinkle the tomato, cheddar, and avocado over the rice and after that cowl once more till the point while the cheddar softens, round 2 minutes. At that factor sprinkle with green onion and cilantro and serve

Nutritional Information per Serving

Calories: 321g, Fat 13g, Carbs 29g, Sugar 5g, Protein 23g

Points Values: 5

RECIPE :- FRIED CHICKEN

Servings: 3

Total Time: 55mins, Prep Time: 10mins, Cook Time: 45mins

Ingredients:

- ❖ ¼ - cup reduced-calorie mayonnaise
- ❖ 1 - teaspoon Dijon mustard
- ❖ 2 - teaspoons grated lemon zest
- ❖ ½ - teaspoon salt
- ❖ 4 - drops hot pepper sauce
- ❖ 3 - ½ - lb chicken, cut into eighths, skin removed
- ❖ ¾ - cup corn flake crumbs

Instructions:

- ✓ Preheat broiler to 375 degrees, splash an extensive shallow preparing container with nonstick shower.
- ✓ Whisk together the initial five fixings in a vast bowl, at that point include the chicken, hurling to coat.
- ✓ Put the cornflake morsels into a substantial zip bolt sack, and include the chicken one piece at once, shaking to coat.
- ✓ Place the chicken in the heating container, splash the highest point of the chicken delicately with nonstick shower, prepare until brilliant dark colored and cooked through around 45 minutes.

Nutritional Information per Serving
Calories: 160.1g, Fat 2.8g, Carbs 28.0g, Sugars 1.9g, Protein 6.0g
Points Values: 5

RECIPE :- SPAGHETTI & CHICKEN MEATBALLS

Servings: 6

Total Time: 55mins, Prep time: 20mins, Cook time: 35mins

Ingredients:

- ❖ 1 - pound ground chicken breast
- ❖ 2 - large eggs
- ❖ ½ - cup seasoned dried bread crumbs
- ❖ ½ - cup grated Parmesan
- ❖ ¼ - teaspoon salt
- ❖ 3 - teaspoons olive oil
- ❖ 1 - medium onion, chopped
- ❖ 2 - garlic cloves, minced
- ❖ 1 - teaspoon dried basil
- ❖ 28 -ounces diced tomatoes
- ❖ 3 - tablespoons tomato paste
- ❖ 6 - ounces whole-wheat spaghetti

Instructions:

- ✓ To make the meatballs, in an in-depth bowl delicately combine the bird, eggs, bread pieces, Parmesan and salt till the point that every one round combined. With delicately saturated palms, form the blend into 18 meatballs.
- ✓ Warmth 2 teaspoons of the oil in an expansive nonstick skillet set over medium-excessive warmth.
- ✓ Add the meatballs and cook, turning periodically, till seared, 6-eight minutes. Exchange the meatballs to a plate.
- ✓ Add the rest of the 1 teaspoon oil to the skillet. Include the onion, garlic, and basil and cook, blending at instances, till the factor that the onion starts to decrease, 2-three minutes. Blend inside the tomatoes and tomato glue and warmth to the factor of boiling.
- ✓ Diminish the warm temperature to low and stew, found out, until the point that the sauce thickens marginally, around 10 minutes.
- ✓ Include the meatballs, cowl, and stew till the factor that the meatballs are cooked via, eight-10 minutes longer.
- ✓ In the meantime, prepare dinner the spaghetti as in line with the bundle bearings.

✓ Gap the spaghetti among 6 bowls; top similarly with the meatballs and sauce.

Nutritional Information per Serving

Calories: 351g, Fat 10g, Carbs 37g, Sugar 14g, Protein 30g

Points Values: 8

RECIPE :- GRILLED LEMON CHICKEN BREASTS WITH TARRAGON

Servings: 4

Total Time: 2hrs 10mins, Prep time: 2hrs, Cook time: 10mins

Ingredients:

- ❖ ¼ - cup dry white wine or chicken broth
- ❖ 1 - tablespoon minced fresh tarragon
- ❖ 1 - teaspoon grated lemon zest
- ❖ 2 - tablespoons fresh lemon juice
- ❖ 2 - garlic cloves
- ❖ 4 - boneless skinless chicken breasts
- ❖ Salt and pepper to taste

Instructions:

✓ To set up the marinade, in a gallon-estimate sealable plastic sack, join the wine, tarragon, lemon pizzazz, lemon juice, and garlic. Include the chicken and seal the pack, pressing out the air and swinging to coat the chicken. Refrigerate something like 2 hours or medium-term, turning the pack infrequently on the off chance that you can.

- ✓ Shower the oven or barbecue rack with a non-stick cooking splash.
- ✓ Deplete the chicken and dispose of the marinade.
- ✓ Season the chicken with salt and pepper and after that cook or barbecue, until the point that the chicken is done, around 5 minutes for each side.

Nutritional Information per Serving:

Calories: 141g, Fat 1g, Carbs 2g, Sugar 0.3g, Protein 26g

Points Values: 3

RECIPE :- EASY STACKED CHICKEN ENCHILADAS RECIPE

Servings: 4

Total Time: 35mins, Prep time: 15mins, Cook time: 20mins

Ingredients:

- ❖ 1 - cup shredded cooked chicken breast
- ❖ 1 - cup canned black beans, rinsed and drained
- ❖ 1/3 - cup thinly sliced green onions
- ❖ ¼ - cup enchilada sauce
- ❖ ¾ - cup picante sauce
- ❖ 6 -inch corn tortillas
- ❖ 1 - cup shredded low-fat cheddar cheese

Instructions:

- ✓ Preheat stove to 350F degrees.
- ✓ Coat a 9-inch pie container with a nonstick cooking splash and put it aside.
- ✓ In a bowl, mix together the chicken, dark beans and green onions.
- ✓ In a separate bowl, mix together the enchilada and picante sauces.
- ✓ Coat the two sides of one tortilla with the sauce blend and place it in the readied pie plate. Rehash layers twice.
- ✓ Top with outstanding tortilla, sauce, and cheddar.

- ✓ Cover and prepare at 350°F for 20 to 30 minutes, or until warmed through.
- ✓ Cut into wedges and serve.

Nutritional Information per Serving

Calories: 230g, Fat 4.5g, Carbs 24.6g, Sugar 5.6g, Protein 22.9g

Points Values: 5

RECIPE :- CHICKEN BRUNSWICK STEW RECIPE

Servings: 4

Total Time: 1hr, Prep time: 20mins, Cook time: 40mins

Ingredients:

- ❖ 1 - tablespoon all purpose flour
- ❖ ¼ - teaspoon cayenne pepper
- ❖ 4 - boneless skinless chicken breasts
- ❖ 2 - slices center cut bacon
- ❖ 2 - stalks celery
- ❖ 1 - onion
- ❖ 1 - medium red bell pepper
- ❖ 14 to 15 - ounces diced tomatoes
- ❖ 1 - cup chicken broth
- ❖ 2 - cups frozen mixed vegetables
- ❖ 1 - tablespoon apple cider vinegar
- ❖ 1 - teaspoon sugar
- ❖ 1 - bay leaf
- ❖ ½ - teaspoon Worcestershire sauce
- ❖ 1/8 - teaspoon hot pepper sauce

Instructions:

- ✓ In a medium bowl, consolidate the flour and cayenne pepper. Add the chook and hurl to coat it with the flour combo.
- ✓ Place the bacon in an extensive pot set over medium warm temperature.

- ✓ Expel the bacon and deplete it on paper towels and positioned it aside. Add the hen to the pot and cook, blending now and again, until the factor that it's far delicately caramelized four to 6mins.
- ✓ Include the celery, onion and ringer pepper to the pot and cook dinner, mixing occasionally, until the factor when the vegetables start to mellow, 4 to 5mins.
- ✓ Mix within the tomatoes and soup, scratching up any flour and different dark-colored bits which have adhered to the base of the skillet.
- ✓ Blend inside the fowl, blended vegetables, vinegar, sugar, clover leaf, Worcestershire sauce, and pepper sauce.
- ✓ Disintegrate the bacon and mix it in as properly.
- ✓ Heat the stew up to the factor of boiling and in a while bring down the warmth and stew, halfway secured, till the point that the veggies are extremely delicate and the stew has thickened, 20 to 25 minutes.
- ✓ Expel the inlet leaf and do away with it. Taste and consist of more salt, pepper and warm pepper sauce as wanted.

Nutritional Information per Serving

Calories: 268g, Fat 6g, Carbs 17g, Sugar 5g, Protein 36g

Points Values: 6

RECIPE :- MINI BUFFALO CHICKEN BITES

Servings: 11

Total Time: 27mins, Prep time: 15mins, Cook time: 12mins

Ingredients:

- ❖ 4 - ounces reduced fat cream cheese
- ❖ 1 - tablespoon cayenne pepper sauce
- ❖ 10 - ounces diced tomatoes
- ❖ 5 - ounces chunk chicken breast
- ❖ ½ - cup shredded reduced fat cheddar cheese
- ❖ 22 - frozen mini fillo shells
- ❖ 1 - stalk celery

Instructions:

- ✓ Warmth stove to 350°F. Place the cream cheddar and pepper sauce in a medium microwave-safe bowl. Cover and microwave on HIGH for 30 seconds and after that mix until smooth.
- ✓ Include the depleted tomatoes, chicken and destroyed cheddar, Stir well, separating any vast bits of chicken, until the point that very much mixed.
- ✓ Partition the blend uniformly between the filled shells. Place on a vast shallow preparing container. Prepare 8 to 12 minutes or until warmed through.

Nutritional Information per Serving
Calories: 75g, Fat 4.8g, Carbs 5.4g, Sugar 2.1g, Protein 4.2g
Points Values: 3

RECIPE :- BAKED CHICKEN PARMESAN

Servings: 8

Total Time: 40mins, Prep Time: 10mins, Cook Time: 30mins

Ingredients:

- ❖ 4- Chicken breast, sliced in half lengthwise to make 8
- ❖ ¾ - cup seasoned breadcrumbs
- ❖ ¼ - cup grated Parmesan cheese
- ❖ 2 - Tbsp butter
- ❖ ¾ - cup reduced fat mozzarella cheese
- ❖ 1 - Cup marinara
- ❖ Cooking spray

Instructions:

- ✓ Preheat broiler to 450°F. Splash an extensive preparing sheet daintily with shower.
- ✓ Join breadcrumbs and parmesan cheddar in a bowl. Liquefy the spread in another bowl. Delicately brush the spread onto the chicken, and after that plunge into breadcrumb blend. Place on heating sheet and rehash with the staying chicken.
- ✓ Daintily shower somewhat more oil to finish everything and prepare in the broiler for 25 minutes.
- ✓ Expel from stove, spoon 1 tbsp sauce over each bit of chicken and best each with 1/2 tbsp of destroyed mozzarella cheddar.
- ✓ Heat 5 more minutes or until the point that cheddar is softened.

Nutritional Information per Serving

Calories: 251g, Fat 9.5g, Crabs 14g, Sugar 0.3g, Protein 31.5g

Points Values: 4

RECIPE :- BUBBLE UP CHICKEN POT PIE

Servings: 8

Total Time: 47mins, Prep Time: 10mins, Cook Time: 37mins

Ingredients:

- ❖ 2 - tablespoons butter
- ❖ 3 - tablespoons flour

- ❖ 2 ½ - cups of low sodium chicken
- ❖ ½ - cup of milk
- ❖ 1 - cup of frozen mixed vegetables
- ❖ 2 – 3 - cups of shredded chicken
- ❖ Salt to taste & Pepper to taste
- ❖ ¼ - teaspoon of crushed red pepper
- ❖ 16.5 - oz low fat buttermilk biscuits

Instructions:

- ✓ Soften margarine in huge stockpot. Include every one of the vegetables and cook until the point that the onions are straightforward.
- ✓ Sprinkle some salt, pepper, and 1/4 teaspoon of pounded red pepper on the vegetables.
- ✓ Cook for around 5-10 minutes.
- ✓ Include flour and cook for 2 minutes.
- ✓ Next, and in chicken stock and blend until the point when the blend turns out to be thick.
- ✓ Blend in 1/2 some drain and include the chicken. Pour the chicken and vegetable blend into a 9 X 13 in goulash and layer on the scones. Heat at 350 for 25 minutes

Nutritional Information per Serving:

Calories: 336g, Fat 9.5g, Crabs 41.56g, Sugar 11.18g, Protein 21.57g

Points Values: 7

RECIPE :- THAI CHICKEN

Total Time: 55mins, Prep Time: 15mins, Cook Time: 40mins

Ingredients:

- ❖ 2 - ½ - tablespoons grated fresh gingerroot
- ❖ 2 - tablespoons chopped garlic
- ❖ 1/8 - teaspoon crushed red pepper flakes
- ❖ 4 - boneless skinless chicken breasts
- ❖ ½ - cup flour
- ❖ salt and pepper
- ❖ 2 - tablespoons olive oil
- ❖ 4 - tablespoons soy sauce
- ❖ ½ - cup brown sugar
- ❖ ½ - cup white wine vinegar
- ❖ 1 - teaspoon fish sauce
- ❖ 1 – Cup sugar snap pea

Instructions:

- ✓ Blend flour with salt and pepper to flavor and dig bird pieces in this.
- ✓ Warmth the olive oil in an extensive skillet.
- ✓ Sauté the hen until seared on the 2 aspects and cooked through.
- ✓ Expel the chook and put in a warm dish, positioned aside in low stove to preserve warm.
- ✓ Add the ginger-garlic combination to the skillet and sauté until daintily sautéed.
- ✓ Include the soy sauce, darker sugar, and vinegar and fish sauce.
- ✓ Heat the combination to the point of boiling.
- ✓ Decrease the warm temperature and stew, blending as regularly as viable, till the point that the sauce diminishes and thickens.
- ✓ Pour the sauce over the bird portions inside the warm serving dish and preserve warm till prepared to serve.
- ✓ Trim and shred the sugar snap pea's nook to the corner.
- ✓ Only earlier than serving sprinkle the very best factor of the chicken with the destroyed snap peas.

Nutritional Information per Serving:

Calories: 390g, Fat 17g, Crabs 42g, Sugars 4g, Protein 20g

Points Values: 5

RECIPE :- KOREAN GRILLED CHICKEN BREASTS

Servings: 4

Total Time: 20mins, Prep Time: 10mins, Cook Time: 10mins

Ingredients:

- ❖ 1 - pound boneless
- ❖ ¼ - cup low sodium or gluten-free soy sauce
- ❖ ¼ - cup unsweetened apple sauce
- ❖ ¼ - cup finely chopped yellow onion
- ❖ 1 - tsp sesame oil
- ❖ 1 - tsp grated ginger
- ❖ 1 - tbsp light brown sugar
- ❖ 2 - garlic cloves, crushed
- ❖ 1 - teaspoon red pepper flakes
- ❖ 1 - teaspoon sesame seeds, plus more for topping
- ❖ 2 - thinly sliced scallions, white and green parts

Instructions:

- ✓ Place the chicken bosoms, 1 at any given moment, in a Ziploc sack. Pound the chicken bosom to an even thickness, about ½ inch thick, being mindful so as not to cut the pack.
- ✓ In a medium bowl, join the soy sauce, fruit purée, onion, sesame oil, ginger, dark colored sugar, garlic, red pepper drops, if utilizing and sesame seeds.
- ✓ Hold ¼ measure of the marinade and exchange the rest of the Ziploc sack with the chicken.
- ✓ Refrigerate and marinate for somewhere around 60 minutes.
- ✓ Over medium-high warmth, barbecue the chicken for 2 to 3 minutes or until it never again adheres to the flame broil.
- ✓ Turn the chicken, spoon the held ¼ measure of marinade over each bosom and flame broil an expansion 2 to 3 minutes.

Nutritional Information per Serving

Calories: 180g, Fat 4.5g, Crabs 9g, Sugar 6g, Protein 25g

Points Values: 3

RECIPE :- GRILLED CHICKEN AND BLUEBERRY SALAD

Serving: 4

Total Time: 25mins, Prep Time: 10mins, Cook Time: 15mins

Ingredients:

- ❖ 5 - cups mixed greens
- ❖ 1 - cup blueberries
- ❖ ¼ - cup slivered almonds
- ❖ 2 - cups cubed chicken breasts, cooked

Dressing:

- ❖ ¼ - cup olive oil
- ❖ ¼ - cup apple cider vinegar
- ❖ ¼ - cup blueberries
- ❖ 2 - Tbsp honey
- ❖ salt and pepper to taste

Instructions:

- ✓ In an expansive bowl, hurl the greens, blueberries, almonds, and chicken bosoms until the point that all around blended.

- ✓ For the serving of mixed greens dressing, consolidate the olive oil, apple juice vinegar, blueberries, and nectar in a blender.
- ✓ Mix until smooth. Add salt and pepper to taste.

Nutritional Information per Serving:

Calories: 266g, Fat 17.9g, Carbs 18.0g, Sugars 13.6g, Protein 10.9g

Points Values: 9

RECIPE :- SLOW COOKER CHICKEN GYROS

Servings: 8

Total : 6hrs 50mins, Prep Time: 20mins, Cook Time: 6hrs 30mins

Ingredients:

- ❖ ½ - small onion
- ❖ 3 - cloves garlic
- ❖ 2 - pounds ground chicken
- ❖ 2 - eggs, whisked
- ❖ ½ - cup plain whole wheat breadcrumbs
- ❖ 1 - lemon, juiced and zested
- ❖ 1 - teaspoon dried thyme
- ❖ ¼ - teaspoon cinnamon
- ❖ ¼ - teaspoon nutmeg
- ❖ 2 - teaspoons salt
- ❖ 1 - tablespoon extra virgin olive oil

- ❖ 6- inch whole wheat

Toppings:

- ❖ 1 - tomato
- ❖ 1 – cucumber
- ❖ ½ - cup low-fat plain Greek yogurt
- ❖ 1 - lemon

Instructions:

- ✓ In a sustenance processor, beat onion and garlic till pureed.
- ✓ In an in depth bowl, mixture collectively onion puree, ground hen, eggs, breadcrumbs, lemon, thyme, cinnamon, nutmeg, and salt. Combine till the factor while all around joined.
- ✓ Shape into an expansive ball and region in a four-quart Crockpot which has been sprinkled with olive oil.
- ✓ Cover and cook dinner for 4-6 hours on high, or 6-8 hours on low.
- ✓ Unplug Crockpot and evacuate cover 30 minutes before serving. This will enable the gyros to set and reduce into first-class cuts.
- ✓ At the point newly while prepared to serve, expel meat from mild cooker. Cut and serve on warmed pita bread completed with tomatoes, cucumbers, yogurt, and new crushed lemon juice.
- ✓ Appreciate

Nutritional Information per Serving:

Calories: 248g, Fat 13g, Carbs: 10g, Sugars 2g, Protein 23g

Points Values: 7

Servings: 6

Total Time: 6hrs, Prep Time: 40mins, Cook Time: 5hrs 20mins

Ingredients:

- ❖ 1 - large roasting chicken
- ❖ 2 - teaspoons extra-virgin olive oil
- ❖ 2 - garlic cloves, minced
- ❖ 2 - teaspoons fresh thyme
- ❖ 1 - teaspoon black pepper
- ❖ 1 - teaspoon paprika
- ❖ 1 - teaspoon kosher or sea salt
- ❖ 2 - stalks celery
- ❖ ¼ - cup water (optional)
- ❖ 1 - cup baby carrots
- ❖ 2 - medium potatoes

Instructions:

- ✓ Wash and pat dry hen. Rub the out of doors of a hen with olive oil. Consolidate flavors and rub outwardly of the bird. Place minced garlic inside the hole alongside really greater salt and pepper.
- ✓ Add water to the mild cooker, subsequent the celery and the chook to finish the entirety, bosom facet up. The celery maintains the hen from sautéing plenty on the bottom.
- ✓ Utilize a meat thermometer to test for doneness or pierce with a fork, to ensure the juices run clean.
- ✓ For additional sautéing, precisely expel chook from the mild cooker, put in a considerable simmering container and sear until the factor that coveted shading has been come to.
- ✓ Embellishment bird with new thyme, every time wanted.
Nutritional Information per Serving

Calories: 178g, Fat 8g, Carbs: 15g, Sugars 2g, Protein 10 g

Points Values: 2

Servings: 10

Total Time: 4hrs 30mins, Prep Time: 30mins, Cook Time: 4hrs

Ingredients:

- ❖ 4-6 - boneless, skinless, chicken breasts
- ❖ 2 - 14.5 oz can diced tomatoes
- ❖ 1 - medium onion thinly sliced
- ❖ 4 - garlic cloves
- ❖ ½ - cup balsamic vinegar1 - tablespoon olive oil
- ❖ 1 - teaspoon dried oregano
- ❖ 1 - teaspoon dried basil
- ❖ 1 - teaspoon dried rosemary
- ❖ ½ - teaspoon thyme
- ❖ ground black pepper and salt to taste

Instructions:

- ✓ Pour the olive oil on base of moderate cooker, include chicken bosoms, salt and pepper each bosom, put cut onion over chicken at that point put in all the dried herbs and garlic cloves.
- ✓ Pour in vinegar and best with tomatoes.
- ✓ Cook on high 4hr serve over holy messenger hair pasta.

Nutritional Information per Serving:

Calories: 238g, Fat 12g, Carbs: 7g, Sugar 4g, Protein 25g

Points Values: 1

Servings: 2

Total Time: 15mins, Prep Time: 5mins, Cook Time: 10mins

Ingredients:

- ❖ 8 - oz boneless skinless chicken breast
- ❖ ½ - tsp reduced sodium Montreal Chicken Seasoning
- ❖ cooking spray
- ❖ 2 - cups chopped Romaine lettuce
- ❖ 2 - small tomatoes
- ❖ 1 - corn on the cob with the husk
- ❖ 2 - tbsp Skinny Ranch Dressing
- ❖ 1 - tbsp BBQ Sauce

Instructions:

- ✓ Season the fowl with Montreal fowl flavoring. Cook chook on a flame broil or barbecue skillet showered with oil over medium warmth for around 5mins on each facet, or until the point when the chook is cooked through inside the interior.
- ✓ Exchange to a slicing board and reduce thin.
- ✓ Place the corn inside the microwave for 4mins. Strip the husk of the corn, at that point reduce the corn off the cob.
- ✓ Partition the lettuce, tomatoes, corn, and chicken on two plates, at that factor sprinkle with BBQ Sauce and dressing.

Nutritional Information per Serving:

Calories: 241g, Fat 5g, Carbs 22g, Sugar 7g, Protein 30g

Points Values: 6

Servings: 6

Total Time: 37mins, Prep Time: 12mins, Cook Time: 25mins

Ingredients:

- ❖ 8 - oz uncooked wheat
- ❖ 1 - ½ - cups water
- ❖ 1 - cup skim milk
- ❖ 1 - teaspoon salt
- ❖ ½ - teaspoon dry mustard powder
- ❖ 2 - cups fresh broccoli florets
- ❖ 2 - medium carrots
- ❖ ½ - cup frozen corn kernels
- ❖ 8 - oz cooked boneless
- ❖ 4 – oz. sharp Cheddar cheese

Instructions:

- ✓ Place the dry pasta in an extensive saute dish or profound skillet and pour in the water and drain. Mix in the salt and mustard powder and best with the broccoli, carrots and corn.
- ✓ Turn the warmth on to medium and remain by the stove, blending infrequently and observing nearly for the substance to start to stew.
- ✓ Make beyond any doubt you don't meander away, you don't need the substance to bubble and overflow or for the drain to get overheated and isolated.

- ✓ Cook the blend on low, mixing each couple minutes, for 15-20 minutes until the point when the fluid is generally ingested.
- ✓ Add the cooked chicken pieces and blend in until the point that all around consolidated and cook for another 1-2 minutes. Expel from warmth and mix in the destroyed cheddar.
- ✓ Cover the skillet with a cover for 2-3 minutes until the point that the cheddar is liquefied and afterward blend until the point that very much consolidated and mushy.
- ✓ Serve warm.

Nutritional Information per Serving:

Calories: 395.9g, Fat 6.3g, Carbs 52.3g, Sugars 3.2g, Protein 35.7g

Points Values: 5

Servings: 8

Total Time: 35mins, Prep Time: 15mins, Cook Time: 20mins

Ingredients:

- ❖ 2 - tbsp flour
- ❖ 2 - tbsp parmesan cheese
- ❖ 1/2 - tsp salt
- ❖ ¼ - tsp pepper
- ❖ 16 - oz chicken breast
- ❖ 1 - tbsp olive oil
- ❖ 2 - cup onion
- ❖ 2 - garlic cloves
- ❖ 2 - cup mushrooms
- ❖ ½ - tsp basil
- ❖ 2 - tbsp dry white wine
- ❖ 2 - tbsp water

Instructions:

- ✓ On a sheet of wax paper or paper plate, join flour, parmesan cheddar, and 1/4 tsp each salt and pepper.
- ✓ Dig chicken in flour blend, covering the two sides, and hold any residual flour blend.
- ✓ In a 10 inch skillet, warm 1/2 tsps oil over medium-high warmth; include onions and garlic and saute until the point when onions are relaxed.
- ✓ Include mushrooms, basil, and remaining 1/4 tsp salt and saute until the point that mushrooms are delicate, around 5 minutes.

- ✓ Exchange blends to plate and put aside.
- ✓ In a similar skillet, warm residual 1/2 tsp oil; include chicken and cook, turning once, until softly sautéed, 1 to 2 minutes on each side.
- ✓ Mix in saved flour blend; bit by bit include wine and water and proceeding to mix, heat blend to the point of boiling.
- ✓ Return mushroom blend to the container and cook until warmed through.

Nutritional Information per Serving:

Calories: 338.6g, Fat 8.9g, Carbs 14.9g, Sugars 2.8g, Protein 43.0g

Points Values: 7

RECIPE :- CHICKEN MARSALA

Servings: 4

Total Time: 33mins, Prep Time: 15mins, Cook Time: 18mins

Ingredients:

- ❖ 2 - tsp olive oil
- ❖ 1 - cup fresh mushrooms, sliced
- ❖ 1 - lb boneless skinless boneless, skinless chicken breast, (four 4 oz pieces)
- ❖ 1 - tsp dried thyme
- ❖ ½ - tsp table salt, (more or less to taste)
- ❖ 1/4 - tsp black pepper
- ❖ ½ - cup marsala wine
- ❖ 1 – ¼ - cup reduced-sodium beef broth, divided

- ❖ 1 – ½ - tbsp corn starch

Instructions:

- ✓ Warmth oil in an expansive skillet over medium-high warmth. Include mushrooms and sauté until delicate and discharging fluid, around 5 minutes.
- ✓ In the interim, put chicken on a plate and season the two sides with thyme, salt, and pepper. Move mushrooms to the external edge of skillet once cooked. Place the chicken in focus of skillet and sauté until brilliant, around 2 to 3 minutes for every side.
- ✓ Add wine to skillet; stew 1 minute. Include 3/4 measure of soup and stew, revealed until the point when chicken is delicate and cooked through, around 8 minutes.
- ✓ Break down cornstarch in outstanding 1/2 measure of stock in a little bowl; add to skillet.
- ✓ Stew until the point when sauce thickens, mixing always and consolidating mushrooms into the fluid, around 1 minute.
- ✓ Serve chicken with mushroom sauce spooned over best.

Nutritional Information per Serving:

Calories: 289g, Fat 5g, Carbs 8g, Sugars 2g, Protein 25g

Points Values: 4

Servings: 6

Total Time: 25mins, Prep Time: 10mins, Cook Time: 15mins

Ingredients

- ❖ 1 - cooking spray
- ❖ 4 - large egg white
- ❖ ½ - cup scallion, chopped
- ❖ 2 - medium garlic cloves
- ❖ 12 oz boneless skinless boneless
- ❖ ½ - cup carrot
- ❖ 2 - cup cooked brown rice
- ❖ ½ - cup frozen green peas
- ❖ 3 - tbsp low-sodium soy sauce

Instructions:

- ✓ Coat an extensive nonstick skillet with cooking splash and set dish over medium-high warmth. Include egg whites and cook, until mixed, mixing regularly, around 3 to 5 minutes; expel from container and put aside.
- ✓ Off-warm, recoat skillet with cooking shower and place back over medium-high warmth. Include scallions and garlic; sauté 2 minutes. Include chicken and carrots; sauté until the point that chicken is brilliant darker and cooked through, around 5 minutes.
- ✓ Blend in saved cooked egg whites, cooked darker rice, peas and soy sauce; cook until warmed through, mixing a few times, around 1 minute.

Nutritional Information per Serving
Calories: 179g, Fat 2g, Carbs 21g, Sugars 2g, Protein 18g
Points Values: 4

Servings: 4

Total Time: 31mins, Prep Time: 20mins, Cook Time: 11mins

Ingredients:

- ❖ 2 - tbsp sesame seeds, raw
- ❖ 1 - tbsp water
- ❖ 1 - tbsp low-sodium soy sauce
- ❖ 1 - tbsp maple syrup
- ❖ 1 - tbsp dry sherry
- ❖ 1 - tsp fresh ginger root, minced
- ❖ ½ - tsp five-spice powder spices
- ❖ 2 - tbsp all-purpose flour
- ❖ ½ - tsp salt
- ❖ ¼ - tsp black pepper
- ❖ 1 - lb uncooked boneless skinless boneless
- ❖ 2 - tsp peanut oil

Instructions:

- ✓ Place a vast nonstick skillet over medium-high warmth. Include sesame seeds and cook until delicately toasted, shaking skillet often, around 2 to 3 minutes; exchange seeds to a shallow dish and put aside.
- ✓ Whisk water, soy sauce, maple syrup, sherry, ginger and five-flavor powder together in a little bowl; put aside.
- ✓ Consolidate flour, salt and pepper together in a shallow dish; add chicken and swing to coat. Shake chicken pieces to expel overabundance flour.
- ✓ Warmth oil in a huge nonstick skillet over medium-high warmth. Include chicken and sauté until seared on all

sides, around 5 minutes. Add soy sauce blend to chicken and cook until the point that sauce thickens and is nearly dissipated, around 2 to 3 minutes more.

✓ Plunge chicken pieces in toasted sesame seeds and serve, showered with any extra soy sauce blend.

Nutritional Information per Serving

Calories: 216g, Fat 6g, Carbs 8g, Sugars 3g, Protein 28g

Points Values: 5

RECIPE :- SWORDFISH PASTA STIR FRY

Servings: 4

Total Time: 25mins, Prep Time: 10mins, Cooking time: 15mins

Ingredients:

- ½ - package Penne noodles
- 1 – Tbs. cornstarch
- 2 8 -oz. bottles clam juice
- 2 – Tbs. vegetable oil
- 12 - oz swordfish
- 3 – Tbs. minced fresh ginger root
- 5 - cloves garlic
- 8 - oz sugar snap peas
- 3 - cups cherry tomatoes
- 3 – Tbs. low-sodium soy sauce
- Freshly ground black pepper to taste

Instructions:

- ✓ Get prepared pasta as in keeping with package deal bearings.
- ✓ While Pasta is cooking, whisk together the cornstarch and a pair of tablespoons of the mollusk squeeze in a touch bowl.
- ✓ Include swordfish and panfry over high warmth until murky and cooked through.
- ✓ Expel and put aside.

- ✓ Include the peas, ginger, and garlic to the skillet and panfry for 1 minute.
- ✓ Blend in the cornstarch blend and the rest of the shellfish juice. Stew for 2 minutes.
- ✓ At the point when pasta is done, deplete well.
- ✓ Hurl pasta with swordfish blend.
- ✓ Hurl in tomatoes and soy sauce and blend tenderly until hot.
- ✓ Season with pepper to taste and serve.

Nutritional Information per Serving

Calories: 588g, Fat 14.5g, Carbs 79.1g, Sugar 6.6g, Protein 32.9g

Points Values: 5

RECIPE :- CAJUN CATFISH RECIPE

Servings: 4

Total Time: 16mins, Prep Time; 10mins, Cooking Time: 6mins

Ingredients:

- ❖ 4 - Catfish fillets
- ❖ ¼ - cup Buttermilk
- ❖ ½ - cup Yellow cornmeal
- ❖ ½ - tsp cayenne pepper
- ❖ ½ - tsp black pepper
- ❖ 1 - tsp paprika
- ❖ ½ - tsp salt
- ❖ ½ - tsp onion powder
- ❖ ½ - tsp garlic powder

Instructions:

- ✓ Preheat the oven.
- ✓ Delicately splash oven container with cooking shower.
- ✓ Wash the fish fillets and pat dry.
- ✓ Pour the buttermilk over the filets and swing over to totally coat.
- ✓ In a different bowl, combine the rest of the fixings.
- ✓ Take every catfish filet and shake off abundance buttermilk.
- ✓ Place in the cornmeal blend to totally cover each filet and place on grill dish.
- ✓ Place the grill skillet around 4 crawls from the warmth.
- ✓ Cook for around 3 minutes for every side or until done in the inside.

Nutritional Information per Serving

Calories: 259g, Fat 10.4g, Carbs 14.2g, Sugar 1.1g, Protein 26.4g

Points Values: 6

RECIPE :- OVEN FRIED FISH WEIGHT WATCHERS

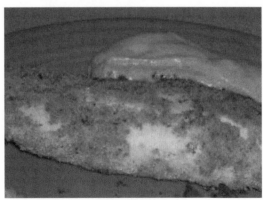

Servings: 6

Total Time: 20mins, Prep Time: 10mins, Cooking: 10mins

Ingredients:

- ❖ 1 ½ - lb fresh haddock, tilapia fillets, or other white fish
- ❖ ¼ - cup white or yellow cornmeal

- ❖ ¼ - cup dry plain or seasoned bread crumbs
- ❖ ½ - tsp dried dill
- ❖ ½ - tsp salt
- ❖ 1/8 - tsp black pepper
- ❖ ½ - tsp paprika
- ❖ 1/3 - cup skim milk
- ❖ 3 - tbsp butter, melted

Instructions:

- ✓ Preheat stove to 450 degrees.
- ✓ In a shallow dish, similar to a pie plate, consolidate every dry fixing.
- ✓ Place drain in another shallow dish.
- ✓ Dunk angle in the drain, at that point in piece blend.
- ✓ Place in a dish covered with a cooling splash.
- ✓ Shower with dissolved margarine.
- ✓ Prepare for 10mins or until the point that angle pieces separated with a fork.

Nutritional Information per Serving

Calories: 196g, Fat 7g, Carb 8g, Sugars 0.3g, Protein 24g

Points Values: 5

RECIPE :- BLACKENED ZUCCHINI WRAPPED FISH

Servings: 4

Total Time: 15mins, Prep Time: 10mins, Cooking Time: 5mins

Ingredients:

- ❖ 2 - zucchinis
- ❖ 24 - oz cod fillets, skin removed
- ❖ 1 - tbsp blackening spices
- ❖ ½ - tbsp olive oil
- ❖ Cooking spray

Instructions:

- ✓ Utilizing a peeler or mandolin, reduce the zucchini into skinny portions the long manner.
- ✓ Season the fish with 1/2 tbsp. Darkening flavoring.
- ✓ Precisely enclose every little bit of fish through the zucchini. Marginally overlaying the zucchini will make this much less disturbing and help it stay installation.
- ✓ Sprinkle the wrapped fish with the relaxation of the darkening zest.
- ✓ Warmth the olive oil in a container sufficiently expansive to preserve the general public of the fish. Include the fish setting accept as true with the closures of the zucchini cuts down first.
- ✓ Cook for 3-four minutes for every aspect or till the point that perspective is flaky and cooked via.

Nutritional Information per Serving

Calories: 186g, Fat 3g, Carbs 5g, Sugars 4g, Protein 37g

Points Values: 4

Serving: 6

Total Time: 52mins, Prep Time: 15mins, Cooking: 37mins

Ingredients:

- ❖ 1 - tbsp olive oil
- ❖ 1 - onion
- ❖ 2 - garlic cloves
- ❖ ¼ - tsp. red pepper flakes
- ❖ 2/3 - cup parsley
- ❖ 3 - tbsp. tomato paste
- ❖ 28 - oz. canned San Marzano tomatoes
- ❖ 8 - oz. clam juice
- ❖ 14 - oz. fish stock
- ❖ 2 - tbsp butter
- ❖ ½ - tsp. oregano
- ❖ ½ - tsp. basil
- ❖ Salt and pepper
- ❖ 1.5 - lbs cod
- ❖ 1 - lb. raw shrimp

Instructions:

- ✓ Warmth the olive oil over medium warmth. Include the onion and cook for 5-7 minutes until starting to end up translucent.

- ✓ Add the garlic and red pepper drops. Cook for 1-2 minutes, mixing frequently. Include the parsley and cook for 1-2 minutes.
- ✓ Mix in the tomato glue and cook for 1 minute.
- ✓ Include the tomatoes, shellfish squeeze, and fish stock. Convey to a stew and include the spread, oregano, and basil.
- ✓ Stew for 10-15 minutes. Now, you need to taste the soup and modify the flavoring as required. Include salt and pepper.
- ✓ If necessary, include additional tomato glue for more tomato season. You can include red pepper drops for more warmth or some additional tomatoes on the off chance that it is excessively hot.
- ✓ Ensure the soup is stewing and include the cod. Cook for 5 minutes. At that point include the shrimp and cook for 4-5 minutes until hazy and cooked through.

Nutritional Information per Serving

Calories: 271g, Fat 7g, Carbs 10g, Sugars 6g, Protein 42g

Points Values: 6

Servings: 4

Total Time: 30mins, Prep Time: 10mins, Cooking Time: 20mins

Ingredients:

- ❖ 1 - 5oz fillet of white fish such as cod
- ❖ 1 - tsp salt
- ❖ 1 - tsp pepper
- ❖ 5 - cherry tomatoes sliced in half
- ❖ 1 - clove garlic thinly sliced
- ❖ 4 - kalamata olives sliced in half
- ❖ 1 - tsp capers
- ❖ 2 - tbsp red onion thinly sliced
- ❖ 2 - tbsp red pepper thinly sliced
- ❖ 1 - tbsp white wine
- ❖ 1 - tbsp lemon juice
- ❖ 1 - tbsp olive oil
- ❖ ½ - tsp red pepper flakes
- ❖ 2 - lemon slices

Instructions:

- ✓ Pre-warm broiler to 400°F. Cut an extensive heart shape from a bit of material paper. Ensure it is sufficiently substantial to accommodate your clench hand in one portion of the heart.
- ✓ Place the fish amidst half of the material paper. Season with salt and pepper and best with cherry tomatoes, garlic, olives, tricks, red onion, and red pepper.

- ✓ Shower olive oil, white wine, and lemon on the fish.
- ✓ Overlap the unfilled half over the other half and seal the sack by squeezing and rolling the edges beginning at the highest point of the heart and consummation at the point. Ensure it is all around fixed.
- ✓ Place on a heating plate and prepare at 400°F for 13 minutes.
- ✓ Expel from broiler and serve quickly clinched. To eat cut a little gap in the best and tear it open.

Nutritional Information per Serving

Calories: 321g, Fat 18g, Carbs 17g, Sugar 5g, Protein 26g

Points Values: 7

RECIPE :- SLIMMING GINGER STEAMED FISH

Servings: 2

Total Time: 27mins, Prep Time: 7mins, Cooking Time: 20mins

Ingredients:

- ❖ 2 - 5oz fillets halibut
- ❖ 1 - tsp salt
- ❖ 3 - scallions julienned
- ❖ 2 - tbsp ginger julienned
- ❖ ½ - red pepper julienned
- ❖ 1 - large clove garlic
- ❖ 1 - tbsp soy sauce
- ❖ 1 ½ - tbsp mirin
- ❖ 1 - tbsp sesame oil
- ❖ ½ - tsp thai chili deseeded

Instructions:

- ✓ In a heatproof bowl that will fit in your steamer put one of the filets and best with half of the salt, scallions, ginger, red peppers and garlic put another filet over the first and rehash the procedure with the rest of the fixings.
- ✓ Include the bean stew, soy sauce, mirin, and sesame oil.

- ✓ In a pot over medium warmth put 1 inch of water in the base of the pot and place steamer in the pot.
- ✓ Place the bowl with the fish in the steamer and cover the pot.
- ✓ Steam the fish for 15-20 minutes relying upon the thickness of your files.
- ✓ Present with darker rice and a large portion of a lemon.

Nutritional Information per Serving

Calories: 233g, Fat 9g, Carbs 8g, Sugar 4g, Protein 28g

Points Values: 5

RECIPE :- ONE PAN BAKED TERIYAKI SALMON

Servings: 4

Total Time: 30mins, Prep Time: 10mins, Cooking Time: 20mins

Ingredients:

- ❖ ½ - cup soy sauce
- ❖ ¼ - cup mirin
- ❖ 2 - tbsp honey
- ❖ ½ - orange juiced
- ❖ 1 - tbsp ginger
- ❖ 2 - cloves garlic
- ❖ ½ - tbsp corn starch
- ❖ 2/3 - cup pineapple
- ❖ ½ - orange
- ❖ ½ - lb salmon fillet
- ❖ 2 - zucchini
- ❖ 2 - carrots
- ❖ 1 - tbsp salt course
- ❖ 1 ½ - tbsp sesame oil
- ❖ 2 - tbsp scallions chopped
- ❖ 1 - tbsp sesame seeds

Instructions:

- ✓ Pre-warm broiler to 400°F.
- ✓ Consolidate the soy sauce, mirin squeezed orange and cornstarch into a pot over medium warmth and heat to the

point of boiling. Lessen warmth and include the pineapple and mix until thick.

✓ Lay the salmon filet skin side down on a preparing sheet canvassed in material paper and slides the orange under the filet midway.

✓ Encompass the outside of the filet with the zucchini and carrot.

✓ Season with salt and the sesame oil and pour the marinade over the salmon filet sparing a little to dress the dish toward the end.

✓ Prepare for 15 minutes at that point sear for 5 minutes or until the point that the best is caramelized.

✓ Enhancement with more sauce, scallions and sesame seeds.

✓ Serve over darker rice and appreciate

Nutritional Information per Serving

Calories: 272g, Fat 8g, Carbs 33g, Sugar 22g, Protein: 18g

Points Values: 4

RECIPE :- SHRIMP SCAMPI

Servings: 4

Total Time: 32mins, , Prep Time: 25mins, Cooking Time: 7mins

Ingredients:

- ❖ 4 - tsp olive oil
- ❖ 1 1/4 - lb medium shrimp , peeled (tails left on)
- ❖ 6 to 8 -garlic cloves, minced
- ❖ ½ - cup low-sodium chicken broth
- ❖ ½ - cup dry white wine
- ❖ ¼ - cup fresh lemon juice
- ❖ ¼ - cup plus 1 tablespoon fresh parsley, minced
- ❖ ¼ - tsp salt
- ❖ ¼ - tsp black pepper, freshly ground
- ❖ 4 - slice lemon

Instructions:

- ✓ In a huge nonstick skillet, warm the oil. Sauté the shrimp until simply pink, 2-3 minutes.
- ✓ Include the garlic and cook mixing always around 30 seconds.
- ✓ With an opened spoon exchange the shrimp to a platter, keep hot.
- ✓ In the skillet, join the juices, wine, lemon juice, 1/some the parsley, the salt, and pepper; heat to the point of boiling.
- ✓ Bubble, revealed, until the point when the sauce is diminished significantly; spoon over the shrimp.
- ✓ Serve decorated with the lemon cuts and sprinkled with the rest of the tablespoon of parsley.

Nutritional Information per Serving

Calories: 184g, Fat 6g, Carbs 6g, Sugars 1g, Protein 21g

Points Values: 4

RECIPE :- BLACKENED FISH TACOS WITH CABBAGE MANGO SLAW

Servings: 4

Total Time: 30mins, Prep Time: 10mins, Cooking Time: 20mins

Ingredients:

For the cabbage slaw:

- ❖ 3 ½ - cups red cabbage
- ❖ 1 - mango
- ❖ 2 - tsp olive oil
- ❖ ¼ - cup cilantro
- ❖ ½ - tsp kosher salt
- ❖ 1 -lime juiced

For the tacos:

- ❖ 1 - tsp smoked paprika

- ❖ 1 - tsp kosher salt
- ❖ ½ - tsp dry mustard
- ❖ ¼ - tsp ground cayenne pepper
- ❖ ¼ - tsp ground cumin
- ❖ ¼ - tsp ground oregano
- ❖ 1/8 - tsp black pepper
- ❖ 1 - lb skinless cod
- ❖ ½ - lime juiced
- ❖ cooking spray
- ❖ 8 - corn tortillas
- ❖ lime wedges for serving
- ❖ ½ - lime

Instructions:

- ✓ Join all the slaw fixings and refrigerate.
- ✓ Blend the dried flavors and flavoring together in a little bowl, crush the lime on the fish at that point rub the flavoring onto the angle.
- ✓ Warmth a solid metal skillet on barbecue or stove on high warmth till extremely hot.
- ✓ Cook angle until the point that dark in the middle and all around sautéed outwardly, around 5 minutes on each side.
- ✓ Warmth the corn tortillas on the flame broil until the point that they somewhat singe, around 1 to 2 minutes.
- ✓ Cut the fish into 8 pieces.
- ✓ Partition the fish similarly between 8 tortillas and best each with 1/2 glass slaw. Present with lime wedges.

Nutritional Information per Serving

Calories: 278g, Fat 5g, Carbs 31g, Sugar 12g, Protein 29g

Points Values: 4

Servings: 2

Total Time: 22mins, Prep Time: 7mins, Cooking Time: 15mins

Ingredients:

- ❖ 8 - oz sole fillet
- ❖ 1 - tbsp
- ❖ 1 ½ - tsp
- ❖ 1 - tsp
- ❖ 2 - tbsp
- ❖ cooking spray

Instructions:

- ✓ Preheat broiler to 450 degrees F.
- ✓ Mastermind filet in an 11 x 7-inch heating dish covered with a cooling splash.
- ✓ Consolidate mustard, lemon juice, and Worcestershire sauce, mixing admirably; spread blend equitably over filet.
- ✓ Sprinkle breadcrumbs equally over fish.
- ✓ Prepare revealed for 12 minutes or until the point that angle pieces effectively when tried with a fork.
- ✓ Sliced filet down the middle and serve instantly.

Nutritional Information per Serving

Calories: 125g, Fat 2g, Carbs 6g, Sugar 1g, Protein 21g

Points Values: 2

Servings: 4

Total Time: 35mins, Prep Time: 15mins, Cook Time: 20mins

Ingredients:

- ❖ 1 - cup uncooked brown rice
- ❖ 1 ¾ - cup water
- ❖ 1.25 -lbs. mahi mahi, skin removed
- ❖ ¼ - teaspoon chipotle chili powder
- ❖ 1 - teaspoon garlic powder
- ❖ 1 - teaspoon smoked paprika
- ❖ ½ - teaspoon salt
- ❖ ¼ - teaspoon ground black pepper
- ❖ 1 - tablespoon canola oil
- ❖ 2 - avocados, mash
- ❖ 2 - tablespoons lime juice
- ❖ 2 - cups purple cabbage, sliced
- ❖ 1 - cup of sliced jicama
- ❖ 1 - cup diced roma tomatoes
- ❖ Picked Onions

Cilantro Lime Dressing:

- ❖ 1 - tablespoon red onion
- ❖ 1 - garlic clove
- ❖ 1 - cup fresh cilantro
- ❖ ¼ - cup canola oil
- ❖ 2 - tablespoons fresh lime juice
- ❖ 2 - tablespoons red wine vinegar
- ❖ 1 - tablespoon honey
- ❖ 2 - teaspoons Dijon mustard
- ❖ ¼ - teaspoon of sea salt
- ❖ pinch of ground cumin

Instructions:

- ✓ Add water and rice to a microwave secure bowl and cowl. Cook in microwave on HIGH for 10 minutes.
- ✓ Let sit down to chill and later on cushion with a fork.

- ✓ In a touch bowl, consist of chipotle bean stew powder, garlic powder, smoked paprika, half teaspoon of salt, and 1/4 teaspoon of dark pepper.
- ✓ Season the fish dry and rub flavor blend on the 2 aspects of the fish.
- ✓ Warmth large skillet to medium-high warmth. Include 1 tablespoon of canola oil to the container, at that factor tenderly region organized fish in skillet. Burn on the two aspects for four-five minutes. Expel from the dish and permit relaxation.
- ✓ To sustenance, the processor includes pink onion, garlic clove, crisp cilantro, 1/a few canola oil, lime juice, crimson wine vinegar, nectar, Dijon mustard, 1/4 teaspoon salt, and cumin. Mix until easy. Put apart.
- ✓ In a touch bowl, encompass beaten avocado and a pair of tablespoons of lime juice. Season with salt to flavor.
- ✓ Blend everything together.
- ✓ Amass the dishes: include 1/2 degree of rice, one filet of fish, a liberal scoop of avocado overwhelm, 1/2 container purple cabbage, 1/4 measure of cut jacamar, 1/4 measure of diced tomato. Shower with dressing blend and serve

Nutritional Information per Serving

Calories: 558g, Fat 26g, Carbs 41g, Sugar 9g, Protein 39g

Points Values: 4

RECIPE :- COCONUT FRIED FISH

Servings: 3

Total Time: 30mins, Prep Time: 10mins, Cooking Time: 20mins

Ingredients:

- ❖ 1 - egg
- ❖ 2 - T pineapple juice
- ❖ 2/3 - c flour
- ❖ 1 ½ - cups shredded coconut, more as needed
- ❖ 5 - snapper fillets
- ❖ Vegetable oil, for frying

Instructions:

- ✓ In a wide, shallow bowl, beat collectively the egg and pineapple juice. Spread the flour and the coconut on isolated plates, reasonable for digging.
- ✓ Include 2-three T vegetable oil to a saute box set over medium warmth.
- ✓ Get the fish filets dry but much as could be anticipated.
- ✓ Dig first inside the flour, at that factor plunge in egg and coat angle in coconut.
- ✓ Working with 2-3 filets straight away, add the fish to the dish. At the point while coconut starts off evolved to dark colored, painstakingly turn over.
- ✓ At the factor while the angle is cooked, expel from skillet. Add more oil to the dish if crucial and rehash with the rest of the fish.
- ✓ Serve quickly.

Nutritional Information per Serving

Calories: 1366g, Fat 102g, Carbs 32g, Sugars 4g, Protein 82g

Points Values: 5

Servings: 3

Total Time: 35mins, Prep Time: 10mins, Cook Time: 25mins

Ingredients:

- ❖ Fish
- ❖ 500g - firm white fish fillet
- ❖ 1 - tbsp lime juice
- ❖ ¼ - tsp salt
- ❖ Black pepper
- ❖ 1 - tbsp olive oil
- ❖ Broth
- ❖ 1 ½ - tbsp olive oil
- ❖ 2 - garlic cloves , minced
- ❖ 1 - small onion , finely diced
- ❖ 1 - large red bell pepper
- ❖ 1 ½ - tsp sugar
- ❖ 1 - tbsp cumin powder
- ❖ 1 - tbsp paprika
- ❖ 1 - tsp cayenne pepper
- ❖ ½ - tsp salt
- ❖ 400ml - coconut milk
- ❖ 400ml - canned crushed tomatoes
- ❖ 1 - cup fish broth
- ❖ Finishes
- ❖ 1 - tbsp lime juice
- ❖ 3 - tbsp roughly chopped fresh cilantro

Instructions:

- ✓ Fish:
- ✓ Consolidate the fish, lime squeeze, salt, and pepper in a bowl. Cover with stick wrap and refrigerate for 20 mins.
- ✓ Warmth the 1 tbsp olive oil in a big skillet over excessive warmth.
- ✓ Include the fish and cook till the factor that definitely cooked via and mild superb darker. Expel from the skillet and placed apart.
- ✓ **Soup:**
- ✓ Decrease the stove to medium-excessive and heat 1/2 tbsp olive oil in a comparable skill set.

- ✓ Include the garlic and onion and cook for half minutes or until the factor when the onion is starting to grow to be translucent.
- ✓ Include the Chile peppers and cook for 2 minutes.
- ✓ Include the relaxation of the Broth fixings. Convey to stew, at that point swing all the way down to medium.
- ✓ Cook for 15 to twenty mins or until the point that it thickens. Modify salt and pepper to taste.
- ✓ Restore the fish to the juices to warm - around 2 minutes.
- ✓ Blend thru lime juice.
- ✓ Enhancement with cilantro/coriander and gift with rice.

Nutritional Information per Serving

Calories: 360.6g, Fat 22.5g, Carbs 13.5g, Sugars 0.2g, Protein 12.5g

Points Values: 5

RECIPE :- BLACKENED CATFISH OVER CAJUN RICE RECIPE

Servings: 6

Total Time: 55mins, Prep Time: 10mins, Cooking Time: 45mins

Ingredients:

For the catfish:

- ❖ 2 - catfish filets
- ❖ 2-3 - tablespoons old bay
- ❖ 2 - tablespoons olive oil

For the Cajun rice:

- ❖ 1 - cup brown rice
- ❖ 1 ½ - cups water
- ❖ 2 - tablespoons olive oil
- ❖ 1-2 - cloves garlic, minced
- ❖ ½ - cup chopped green bell pepper
- ❖ ½ - cup chopped white onion
- ❖ ½ - teaspoon garlic powder
- ❖ 2 - teaspoon Cajun seasoning

❖ salt and pepper to taste

Instructions:

- ✓ Bring 1/some water to a bubble in a sauce dish and mix in the rice, diminish warmth to a stew and cover.
- ✓ Let stew until the point when rice is delicate and fluid has consumed around 45 minutes. Put rice aside.
- ✓ While rice is cooking, cover catfish filets with darkening flavoring, totally covering the two sides.
- ✓ Warmth olive oil (subsidiary connection) in a skillet over medium warmth, singe catfish, around 3-4 minutes for every side or until white and flakey.
- ✓ Place angle on a plate and cover with tinfoil to keep warm, put aside.
- ✓ Flush the skillet and include another 2 tablespoons of olive oil (associate connection) over medium warmth. Include the garlic, ringer pepper, and onion.
- ✓ Sauté until the point when fragrant and vegetables are delicate, around 5-7 minutes.
- ✓ Deplete the rice when prepared, include sautéed vegetables and blend in the garlic powder, Cajun flavoring, salt, and pepper.
- ✓ Serve the catfish filets over rice and enhancement with a lemon wedge and appreciate

Nutritional Information per Serving

Calories: 249.7g, Fat 11.7g, Carbs 7.4g, Sugars 4.9g, Protein 28.3g

Points Values: 7

RECIPE :- SPINACH AND FETA STUFFED TILAPIA

Servings: 6
Total Time: 40mins, Prep Time: 15mins, Cook Time: 25mins

Ingredients:

- ❖ 15-16 - oz. tilapia fillets 6 thin fillets
- ❖ Pinch of salt and pepper
- ❖ 1 - egg beaten
- ❖ ½ - cup part-skim ricotta cheese
- ❖ ½ - cup crumbled feta cheese
- ❖ ½ - cup bread crumbs
- ❖ 1 - cup fresh spinach leaves chopped
- ❖ ¼ - tsp. salt
- ❖ ¼ - tsp. ground black pepper
- ❖ ¼ - tsp. dried thyme leaves
- ❖ 1 - large lemon

Instructions:

- ✓ Preheat stove to 350 degrees F.
- ✓ Splash a 2 quart heating dish with cooking shower. Pat fish dry with paper towels and sprinkle each with a spot of salt and pepper.
- ✓ In a little bowl, blend the egg with the ricotta until smooth.
- ✓ Add the feta, bread pieces, spinach, ¼ tsp. salt, 1/4 tsp. dark pepper, and thyme.
- ✓ Partition the filling between the fish filets, setting the filling on the amplest end of the filet. Roll the fish around the filling.
- ✓ Secure the crease with toothpicks, if necessary.
- ✓ Place the stuffed fish, crease side down in the heating dish. Crush the juice of 1 lemon over the highest point of the stuffed fish.
- ✓ Cover and prepare for 25 minutes. The stuffing ought to be cooked through and the fish should drop when contacted with a fork.

Nutritional Information per Serving

Calories: 181g, Fat 6.9g, Carbs 8.5g, Sugar 4.8g, Protein 21.4g

Points Values: 6

Servings: 4

Total Time: 17mins, Prep Time: 5mins, Cooking: 12mins

Ingredients:

- ¾ - cup freshly grated Parmesan cheese
- 2 - teaspoons paprika
- 1 - tablespoon chopped parsley
- ¼ - teaspoon salt
- 1 - tablespoon extra virgin olive oil
- 4 - tilapia filets
- lemon

Instructions:

- ✓ Preheat the broiler to 400°F. Line a preparing sheet with thwart.
- ✓ In a shallow bowl, combine the Parmesan, paprika, parsley and salt.
- ✓ Sprinkle the tilapia with the olive oil, at that point dig in the cheddar blend, squeezing it in delicately with your fingers if vital. Exchange to the heating sheet.
- ✓ Prepare until the point when the fish is misty in the thickest section, 10-12 minutes. Present with the lemon cuts.

Nutritional Information per Serving
Calories: 214g, Fat 12g, Carbs 1g, Sugar: 0.3g, Protein 27g
Points Values: 6

Servings: 5

Total Time: 38mins, Prep Time: 15mins, Cooking Time: 23mi

Ingredients:

For the Tilapia:

- ❖ 2 - tablespoons olive oil
- ❖ 1 and ½ - pounds fresh tilapia, cut into 3 or 4 fillets
- ❖ Salt and pepper

For the Tomato Basil Sauce:

- ❖ 2 - tablespoons olive oil
- ❖ ½ - teaspoon crushed red pepper flakes
- ❖ 2 or 3 - cloves garlic
- ❖ 1 - pint cherry tomatoes
- ❖ 1 - small jalapeño
- ❖ ¼ - cup vegetable stock
- ❖ ½ - cup fresh basil
- ❖ 2 - tablespoons fresh lemon juice
- ❖ ½ - teaspoon fresh lemon zest
- ❖ Salt and fresh ground black pepper

Instructions:

For the Tomato Basil Sauce:

- ✓ Warmth oil in a huge sauté container over medium warmth. Include squashed red pepper drops and garlic and sauté for 1 minute, or until the point that garlic is fragrant.

- ✓ Include the cherry tomatoes and jalapeño and cook, blending at times, until they're delicate and ranking, yet at the same time hold their shape, around 12 minutes. Include the vegetable stock, mix, and enable the blend to go to a light stew.
- ✓ Blend in the basil, lemon juice, lemon pizzazz, salt, and pepper and cook for 2 minutes.
- ✓ Move the sauce into an expansive bowl and put aside for some other time

For the Tilapia:

- ✓ Warmth oil in a similar skillet over medium warmth. Season the two sides of fish with salt and pepper. Place tilapia filets in the oil and cook until brilliant darker, around 3 minutes on both sides, until the point that it's cooked through.
- ✓ Pour the tomato basil sauce over the fish and warm rapidly.
- ✓ Serve at the same time without a moment's delay with extra slashed basil and rice, or cauliflower rice, or zucchini noodles. Appreciate

Nutritional Information per Serving

Calories: 150.9g, Fat 8.7g, Carbs 0.1g, Sugars 0.3g, Protein 20.6g

Points Values: 5

Servings: 3
Total Time: 1hr 10mins, Prep Time: 30mins, Cooking Time: 40mins

Ingredients:

- ❖ 1 - kg floury potatoes
- ❖ 3 - tbsp butter
- ❖ 3 - tbsp double heavy cream
- ❖ large pinch of salt and pepper
- ❖ 600ml - full fat milk
- ❖ 2 - boneless salmon fillets
- ❖ 1-2 - boneless cod or haddock fillet
- ❖ 15 - king prawns shrimp these can be cooked or raw
- ❖ 2 - tbsp plain/all-purpose flour
- ❖ 150g - grated mature cheddar cheese

To serve:

- ❖ 1 - tbsp chopped chives
- ❖ Peas
- ❖ Sweet-corn

Instructions:

- ✓ Preheat the range to 200c/400f
- ✓ Place the potatoes into a dish and cover with chilly water. Convey to the bubble and after that stew for 15mins.
- ✓ Deplete the potatoes and after that pound with a potato masher or ricer. Blend in half of the unfolding, the cream and a hint of salt and pepper.
- ✓ Put to the other facet.

- ✓ Place the drain in a massive pot with the salmon filets and the cod/haddock. Convey to the bubble and stew for 2-3mins.
- ✓ At this point, your fish ought to be cooked and starting to piece separated.
- ✓ Place a sifter over a huge bowl and spill out the fish/drain mixture. Put the drain to the alternative aspect. Place the fish onto a plate and piece separated, evacuate and eliminate the skin if the fish wasn't skinless.
- ✓ Separation the chipped fish and prawns between five little pie dishes.
- ✓ On the opposite hand you could make use of one substantial getting ready dish.
- ✓ Give your drain dish a wash and a dry.

The sauce:
- ✓ Liquefy the rest of the un-fold inside the drain field, at that factor blend inside the flour. Warmth thru on medium warmth whilst mixing with a wooden spoon. Gradually include the saved drain which you cooked the fish in even as blending with an inflatable whisk.
- ✓ The sauce will start to thicken following a few minutes. Kill the warm temperature and blend via a massive portion of the cheddar and a hint of darkish pepper.

Nutritional Information per Serving

Calories: 570g, Fat 27g, Carbs 33g, Sugars 6g, Protein 46g

Points Values: 5

Servings: 4

Total Time: 3hrs 25mins, Prep Time: 3hrs 5mins, Cooking Time: 20mins

Ingredients:

- ❖ ¼ - cup minced fresh flat-leaf parsley
- ❖ 2 - tablespoons minced fresh cilantro
- ❖ ½ - cup olive oil
- ❖ 2 - teaspoons sweet Hungarian paprika
- ❖ 8 - threads Spanish saffron
- ❖ 1 - teaspoon ground ginger
- ❖ 1 - lemon
- ❖ 4 - six-ounce boned fish fillets
- ❖ 4 - large tomatoes
- ❖ 2 - large garlic cloves
- ❖ 1 - teaspoon ground cumin
- ❖ Salt and pepper to taste
- ❖ 2 - carrots, peeled, sliced diagonally ¼-inch
- ❖ 1 - onion
- ❖ 1 - tablespoon preserved lemon pulp
- ❖ 12 - green and/or black olives

Instructions:

- ✓ In a huge bowl, blend parsley, cilantro, olive oil, paprika, saffron, and ginger. Include juice of half of the lemon. Coat angle filets with the blend, cover and refrigerate for 1 to 2 hours. Cut another lemon half into 8 thin cuts.
- ✓ Convey substantial sauce container of water to bubble. Drop tomatoes each one in turn into bubbling water and tally to 10. Expel with an opened spoon and cool to room temperature. Strip off the skin.
- ✓ Place strainer over medium bowl. Cut tomatoes in quarters and evacuate seeds over the strainer. With a vast spoon, rub seeds to remove juice into a bowl. Coarsely cleave tomatoes.
- ✓ In an expansive sauce skillet, consolidate tomatoes, their juice, garlic, and cumin. Cook over medium warmth, crushing and mixing once in a while, until the point that

sauce thickens somewhat, 8 to 10 minutes. Season with salt and pepper. Put aside.
- ✓ Preheat broiler to 350 degrees F.
- ✓ Place carrot cuts in a single layer on the base of enameled goulash or Dutch stove. Cover with onion cuts. Spoon tomato sauce over onions. Cover goulash firmly with aluminum thwart, or front of Dutch stove. Prepare in center of broiler for around 30 minutes, until the point that carrots are delicate.
- ✓ Expel from the stove and place angle filets over vegetables. Hold marinade. Spread a little-protected lemon mash on each filet and best every one with 2 cups of lemon.
- ✓ Pour saved marinade around filets and encompass with olives. Return dish to stove and prepare, revealed, for 20 to 25 minutes, until the point that angle is flaky.
- ✓ Spoon some of the sauce over fish. Embellishment with parsley or cilantro takes off. Serve over couscous whenever wanted.

Nutritional Information per Serving

Calories: 302g, Fat 18.5g, Carbs 18.2g, Sugars 2.4g, Protein 19.0g

Points Values: 6

RECIPE :- FRIED WHOLE FISH WITH TOMATILLO SAUCE

Servings: 5

Total Time: 25mins, Prep Time: 10mins, Cooking Time: 15mins

Ingredients:

- ❖ 1 - bunch cilantro
- ❖ 8 - ounces tomatillos
- ❖ ¼ - cup drained jarred pickled jalapeños
- ❖ Kosher salt
- ❖ 3 - cups vegetable oil
- ❖ 1 -1/2–2-pound whole fish
- ❖ Warm tortillas

Instructions:

- ✓ Trim cilantro at the point where it turns out to be more stem-y than verdant; put leaves with delicate stems aside to serve.
- ✓ Coarsely cleave around 1/2 glass worth of stems and place in a blender alongside tomatillos, cured jalapeños, and pickling fluid. Purée until smooth; taste and season sauce with salt and all the more pickling fluid whenever wanted.
- ✓ Warmth oil in a substantially solid metal skillet over high. Exchange fish to a cutting board and pat dry completely with paper towels.
- ✓ With a sharp blade, make cuts transversely on a corner to corner along the body of the fish each 2" on the two sides, chopping the distance down deep down. Season angle liberally all around with salt.
- ✓ At the point when the oil is hot it ought to shine, and when you drop a little bit of tortilla into the oil it should start sizzling quickly grasp the fish immovably by the tail and painstakingly lower, head first, into the skillet, making a point to lay it down far from you.
- ✓ Broil until the point that substance on base side is cooked through and skin is profoundly seared and fresh around 4 minutes.
- ✓ While the fish is searing, utilize a metal spoon to treat within the fish's head with a touch of hot oil intermittently. Utilize tongs and a fish spatula to deliberately turn angle over. Sear until the point when substance on the second side is cooked through and skin is profoundly caramelized and fresh around 4 minutes.
- ✓ Exchange to a wire rack and season the two sides with more salt.
- ✓ Pour tomatillo sauce onto a rimmed platter and tenderly place angle to finish everything. Tuck saved cilantro into the cavity between the fish's head and body and around the fish. Present with tortillas.

Nutritional Information per Serving

Calories: 3.1g, Fat 0.1g, Carbs 0.6g, Sugars 0.4g, Protein 0.1g

Points Values: 7

Servings: 4

Total Time: 26mins, Prep Time: 10mins, Cooking Time: 16mins

Ingredients:

- ❖ 2 - tbsp sunflower oil
- ❖ 1 - onion, finely chopped
- ❖ 2 - tbsp tike masala curry paste
- ❖ 4 - ripe tomatoes
- ❖ 1 - sweet potato
- ❖ 400ml - can coconut milk
- ❖ 100ml - vegetable stock or water
- ❖ 400g - white fish
- ❖ 150g - frozen peas
- ❖ Bunch fresh coriander
- ❖ 1 - lime

Instructions:

- ✓ Warmth the oil in an extensive profound skillet or wok over low warmth. Include the onion and cook for 5 minutes until relaxed.
- ✓ Mix in the curry glue and broil for only a couple of minutes. Gather the tomatoes and sweet potato and hurl into a single unit well.

- ✓ Tip in the coconut drain and the stock or water. Convey to a stew and cook for 8 minutes until the point that the sauce is thickened and the sweet potato is relatively delicate.
- ✓ Mix in the fish pieces and peas and cook for only 2-3 minutes. Expel from the warmth and include the cleaved coriander.
- ✓ Present with pilau rice and a wedge of lime to crush over.

Nutritional Information per Serving

Calories: 435g, Fat 25.8g, Carbs 26.8g, Sugars 9.1g, Protein 25.8g

Points Values: 6

RECIPE :- MEXICAN BAKED FISH

Servings: 6

Total Time: 30mins, Prep Time: 15mins, Cooking Time: 15mins

Ingredients:

- ❖ 1 1/2 - lb cod
- ❖ 1 - cup salsa
- ❖ 1 - cup sharp cheddar cheese, shredded
- ❖ ½ - cup corn chips, coarsely crushed
- ❖ 1 - avocado, peeled, pitted and sliced
- ❖ ¼ - cup sour cream

Instructions:

- ✓ Preheat oven to four hundred tiers F (two hundred levels C). Lightly grease one 8x12 inch baking dish.
- ✓ Rinse fish fillets beneath bloodless water, and pat dry with paper towels. Lay fillets side by facet within the organized baking dish. Pour the salsa over the pinnacle, and sprinkle flippantly with the shredded cheese. Top with the overwhelmed corn chips.
- ✓ Bake, uncovered, inside the preheated oven for 15 minutes, or until fish is opaque and flakes with a fork. Serve topped with sliced avocado and bitter cream.

Nutritional Information per Serving

Calories: 311g, Fat 18g, Carbs 11g, Sugars 2g, Protein 28g

Points Values: 4

RECIPE :- STEAMED FISH WITH LIME AND GARLIC RECIPE

Servings: 5

Total Time: 35mins, Prep time: 20mins, Cook time: 15mins

Ingredients:

For the fish:

- ❖ 1 - Whole barramundi
- ❖ 5 - stalks lemongrass

For the sauce:

- ❖ 1 - good chicken stock
- ❖ 2 - Tbsp finely chopped palm sugar
- ❖ 8 - Tbsp lime juice
- ❖ 6 - Tbsp fish sauce
- ❖ 2 - heads of garlic
- ❖ Thai chilies to taste
- ❖ 20 – 25 - sprigs cilantro
- ❖ 2 - stalks Chinese celery

Instructions:

- ✓ Ensure your fish is scaled and gutted, and after that score
- ✓ the fish with 3 askew cuts on each side of the fish.
- ✓ Remove the best parts of the lemongrass, wound, and stuff
- ✓ the lemongrass into the depression of the fish.
- ✓ Steam the fish over high bubbling water for around 10 - 15
- ✓ minutes relying upon the measure of your fish.
- ✓ In a pot, warm the chicken stock until the point that it
- ✓ reaches boiling point, and after that hurls in the sugar, diminish warmth, and bubble until the point that the sugar is totally disintegrated.
- ✓ Empty the blend into a bowl and put aside.
- ✓ Mince the garlic, chilies, and cilantro, and blend into the
- ✓ chicken stock soup, alongside fish sauce and lime juice. Blend tenderly and afterward trial.
- ✓ Ensure its sharp, and offset with a trace of sweetness.
- ✓ At the point when the fish is completely steamed, exchange
- ✓ it to a serving platter, decorate with a bed of Chinese celery, and place the fish on the platter.
- ✓ Delicately scoop on all the sauce over the fish, putting the
- ✓ vast majority of the garlic and chilies on the highest point of the fish.
- ✓ Ensure you eat with steamed rice

Nutritional Information per Serving

Calories: 189.1g, Fat 1.1g, Carbs 16.7g, Sugars 8.0g, Protein 26.1g

Points Values: 5

RECIPE :- SAUTÉED FLOUNDER WITH MINT AND TOMATOES

Servings: 4

Total Time: 16min, Prep: 8min, Cook: 8min

Ingredients:

- ❖ 2 - cups fresh tomatoes
- ❖ ¼ - cups mint leaves
- ❖ ¼ - cups basil
- ❖ ¾ - tsp table salt
- ❖ ½ - tsp black pepper
- ❖ 1 - pound uncooked flounder fillets
- ❖ 2 - sprays cooking spray
- ❖ 2 - tsp olive oil

Instructions:

- ✓ In a medium bowl, consolidate tomatoes, mint, basil, 1/2 teaspoon salt, and 1/4 teaspoon pepper; put aside. Place angle on a plate; rub done with staying salt and pepper.
- ✓ Coat an extensive skillet with cooking shower; include oil and set over medium-high warmth. At the point when oil just starts to gleam, include angle; cook until the point that angle turns murky in focus, around 5 minutes.
- ✓ Add tomatoes to the same skillet; cook until tomatoes simply begin to discharge dampness, scratching the base of the container to slacken drippings, around 1 to 2 minutes. Spoon tomatoes over fish and serve. Yields around 4 ounces fish and 1/2 container tomatoes for every serving.

Nutritional Information per Serving

Calories: 441.2g, Fat 30.3g, Carbs 14.8g, Sugars 0.2g, Protein 8.3g

Points Values: 4

Servings: 4

Total Time: 13min, Prep: 8min, Cook: 5min

Ingredients:

- ❖ 1 - sprays cooking spray
- ❖ 20 - oz uncooked tilapia fillets
- ❖ ½ - tsp table salt
- ❖ ¼ - tsp black pepper
- ❖ 1 - Tbsp fresh lemon juice
- ❖ 2 - tsp garlic herb seasoning

Instructions:

- ✓ Preheat grill. Coat a shallow broiling container with a cooking splash.
- ✓ Season the two sides of fish with salt and pepper.
- ✓ Exchange fish to arranged dish and shower with lemon juice; sprinkle garlic herb flavoring over best.
- ✓ Sear until the point when the angle is fork-delicate, around 5 minutes. Yields 1 filet for each serving.

Nutritional Information per Serving:

Calories: 169.5g, Fat 7.8g, Carbs 5.0g, Sugars 1.0g, Protein 22.0g

Points Values: 6

Servings: 4

Total Time: 145min, Prep: 10min, Cook: 15min

Ingredients:

- ❖ 3 - Tbsp white miso
- ❖ 1 ½ - Tbsp dark brown sugar
- ❖ 1 - Tbsp sake
- ❖ ½ - fl oz mirin
- ❖ 20 - oz uncooked Atlantic cod
- ❖ 1 - sprays cooking spray
- ❖ 2 - Tbsp uncooked scallions

Instructions:

- ✓ In a little bowl, whisk together miso, sugar, purpose, and mirin; spread over cod. Cover and refrigerate for no less than 2 hours or up to 1 day.
- ✓ Off warmth, coat a flame broil or barbecue dish with cooking shower. Preheat to medium warmth.
- ✓ Expel cod from marinade; put in a fish flame broiling bin and barbecue angle, flipping once, until the point that cod is misty and chips effortlessly with a fork, around 5 to 7 minutes for every side.
- ✓ Serve embellished with scallions.

Nutritional Information per Serving:

Calories: 227.2g, Fat 3.1g, Carbs 15.0g, Sugars 2.2g, Protein 30.0g

Points Values: 5

Servings: 4

Total Time: 40min, Prep: 15min, Cook: 25min

Ingredients:

- ❖ 1 - Tbsp olive oil
- ❖ 1 - medium uncooked shallots
- ❖ 2 - medium cloves garlic cloves
- ❖ ½ - tsp crushed red pepper flakes
- ❖ 1 - Tbsp anchovy paste
- ❖ 28 – oz. canned diced tomatoes
- ❖ 1 - Tbsp canned tomato paste
- ❖ 10 - medium olives
- ❖ 2 - Tbsp capers
- ❖ 16 - oz uncooked farmed skinless salmon fillets

Instructions:

- ✓ Preheat stove to 350°F. Warmth oil in a huge ovenproof skillet over medium warmth.
- ✓ Include shallot, garlic, and pepper pieces; cook, mixing once in a while, until the point that vegetables diminish, 2–3 minutes.
- ✓ Include anchovy glue and cook, mixing, until the point that it dissolves into the skillet, around 1 minute. Include tomatoes and tomato glue; lessen warmth to medium-low and stew until the point that sauce thickens, around 5 minutes.
- ✓ Blend in olives and escapades; expel from warmth.

✓ Settle salmon filets into sauce; spoon some sauce over salmon. Cover skillet; heat until the point when the angle is only hazy in focus, 10–12 minutes.

Nutritional Information per Serving

Calories: 280.9g, Fat 16.2g, Carbs 30.3g, Sugars 3.6g, Protein 7.5g

Points Values: 3

RECIPE :- GRILLED TUNA PROVENCAL

Servings: 4

Total Time: 20min, Prep: 10min, Cook: 10min

Ingredients:

- ❖ 1 - pounds uncooked tuna
- ❖ ¾ - tsp sea salt
- ❖ ¾ - tsp black pepper
- ❖ 2 ½ - cups fresh tomatoes
- ❖ 1 - Tbsp rosemary
- ❖ 2 - cloves, medium garlic cloves
- ❖ 2 - Tbsp fresh parsley
- ❖ 6 -large olives
- ❖ 1 - Tbsp olive oil
- ❖ 3 - sprays cooking spray
- ❖ 2 - fl oz red wine
- ❖ 1/8 - tsp sugar

Instructions:

- ✓ Wash fish and pat dry. Rub 1/4 teaspoon every salt and pepper over fish; positioned apart.
- ✓ In a different bowl, consolidate tomatoes, rosemary, garlic, parsley, olives, oil and remaining half teaspoon every salt and pepper; placed aside.
- ✓ Coat an awesome barbecue container with a cooling splash and set over medium-excessive warm temperature.
- ✓ At the factor whilst the box is highly smoking, cook dinner fish for 2 to 3 minutes for every side for unusual.

- ✓ When fish is cooked, expel it to a serving plate and tent it with aluminum thwart to maintain heat.
- ✓ Include wine, tomato combo, and sugar to the recent container; cook, scratching the base of dish every from time to time, until the point that tomato combination diminishes to around 2 glasses and liquor has cooked off round 2 to three minutes.
- ✓ Expel thwart from fish, meagerly cut it and gift with tomato blend over exceptional.

Nutritional Information per Serving:

Calories: 332.6g, Fat 12.7g, Carbs 24.8g, Sugars 0.9g, Protein 28.4g

Points Values: 4

RECIPE :- LEMON-HERB ROASTED SALMON

Servings: 4

Total Time: 31min, Prep: 16min, Cook: 15min

Ingredients:

- ❖ 1 - sprays cooking spray
- ❖ 1 ½ - pounds uncooked wild pink salmon fillets
- ❖ 1/8 - tsp table salt
- ❖ 1/8 - tsp black pepper
- ❖ 4 - Tbsp fresh lemon juice
- ❖ 1 ½ - Tbsp sugar
- ❖ 1 - Tbsp fresh parsley

- ❖ 1 - Tbsp fresh thyme
- ❖ 1 - tsp lemon zest
- ❖ 1 - tsp minced garlic
- ❖ 1 - tsp fresh oregano

Instructions:

- ✓ Preheat stove to 400°F. Coat a little, shallow preparing dish with cooking shower.
- ✓ Season the two sides of salmon with salt and pepper; put salmon in arranged preparing dish and shower with 2 tablespoons of lemon juice.
- ✓ In a little bowl, whisk together outstanding 2 tablespoons of lemon juice, sugar, parsley, thyme, lemon pizzazz, garlic, and oregano; rush until the point that sugar breaks up and put aside.
- ✓ Broil salmon until nearly done, around 13 minutes; expel from the stove and best with the lemon-herb blend. Come back to broiler and meal until the point when salmon is fork-delicate, around 2 minutes more. Topping with crisp hacked herbs and ground pizzazz, whenever wanted.

Nutritional Information per Serving:

Calories: 118.1g, Fat 6.8g, Carbs 1.0g, Sugars 0.3g, Protein 12.9g

Points Values: 5

Servings: 4

Total Time: 20min, Prep: 8min, Cook: 12min

Ingredients:

- ❖ 2 - sprays cooking spray
- ❖ 3 - Tbsp dry roasted, salted macadamia
- ❖ ¼ - cups dried plain breadcrumbs
- ❖ 2 - Tbsp fresh parsley
- ❖ ¾ - tsp table salt
- ❖ 1 - pounds uncooked Mahi mahi fillets
- ❖ 1 - large egg whites

Instructions:

- ✓ Preheat stove to 450°F. Coat a preparing container with a cooking splash; put skillet in the broiler to warm.
- ✓ Place nuts, panko, parsley (or cilantro) and 1/4 teaspoon salt in a small scale chopper or blender; process until consolidated. Empty morsels into a shallow bowl or plate; put aside.
- ✓ Place angle on a plate; rub 1/2 teaspoon salt all over fish. Plunge angle into egg white; swing to coat. Next, plunge angle into nut blend; swing to coat.
- ✓ Expel container from the stove and place angle on the dish. Cook until the point that the focal point of fish is never again translucent, around 10 to 12 minutes. Serve quickly.

Nutritional Information per Serving

Calories: 194.3g, Fat 9.8g, Carbs 5.6g, Sugars 0.6g, Protein 21.4g

Points Values: 3

Conclusion

Thank you for downloading this book!

You will get a wonderful selection of modern WW smart points recipes for weight loss, healthy living while saving money.

I hope this book was able to help you lose weight! If you enjoyed this book, would you be kind enough to share this book with your family, friends, and or co-workers and leave a review on Amazon. By you leaving an honest review for this book on Amazon you will help guide people on Amazon to know that this book is legit and perhaps it can help them out as well.

Sincerely,

Desmond Silas

Made in the USA
Middletown, DE
08 January 2019